Oxford First Rhyming Dictionary

OXFORD
UNIVERSITY PRESS

OXFORD
UNIVERSITY PRESS

Great Clarendon Street, Oxford, OX2 6DP,
United Kingdom

Oxford University Press is a department of the
University of Oxford. It furthers the University's
objective of excellence in research, scholarship, and education
by publishing worldwide. Oxford is a registered trade
mark of Oxford University Press in the UK and in certain
other countries

Text © John Foster 2003

The moral rights of the author have been asserted

First published 2003
Second edition 2008
This edition 2014

British Library Cataloguing in Publication Data
Data available

ISBN: 978-0-19273559-1

10 9 8 7 6 5 4 3 2 1

Paper used in the production of this book is a natural,
recyclable product made from wood grown in sustainable
forests. The manufacturing process conforms to the
environmental regulations of the country of origin.

Printed in Malaysia by Vivar Printing Sdn Bhd

Acknowledgements:

Designed by Melissa Orrom Swan

Illustrations by Katie Saunders and Charlotte Canty © Oxford
University Press 2003

Illustrations by Mary McQuillan © Mary McQuillan 2003

Oxford First Rhyming Dictionary

OXFORD
UNIVERSITY PRESS

How to use this dictionary

You can use this dictionary to help you to find words that rhyme.

You can also use it to learn how to spell words that belong to the same rhyming family.

The alphabet

The key words in this dictionary are listed in alphabetical order. Find your way around the dictionary and the word you are looking for by using the alphabet down the side of each page.

Key words

A key word is a word you use very often. In this dictionary, the key words are in red. Look up the key word to find other words that rhyme with it.

Rhyme family

A rhyme family is a group of words that end with the same rhyming sound and have the same spelling pattern.

You will find the rhyming sound after the key word.

Example:

key word　　　　　　　**rhyming sound**

breeze　　　　　　　*-eeze*

rhyme family

freeze　　sneeze　　wheeze

Sometimes there are several words from one rhyme family which rhyme with words from another rhyme family.

Example:

-eeze rhymes with -ees
bees　chimpanzees　　knees　　trees

And sometimes there are words that rhyme with the key word but have a different spelling pattern.

Example:

Other words that rhyme with breeze
cheese　　these　　fleas　　teas　　please

Rhymes

There are lots of rhymes throughout the dictionary. Use them as a starting point to write rhymes of your own!

> Stan, Stan, the lollipop man
> Drives a blue and yellow van
> And washes his socks in a frying pan.

Indexes

This dictionary has two indexes. The A to Z Index on page 68 lists every word in this dictionary. The key words are printed in **bold** type. This index will lead you to the page where you will find the rhyming words you are looking for.

The Index of Rhyming Sounds on page 78 lists every rhyming sound in this dictionary. You can look up the sound that you want to make rhymes with and go straight to the key word in the main part of the book.

These are the features of the dictionary:

capital letter | letter | rhyming sound

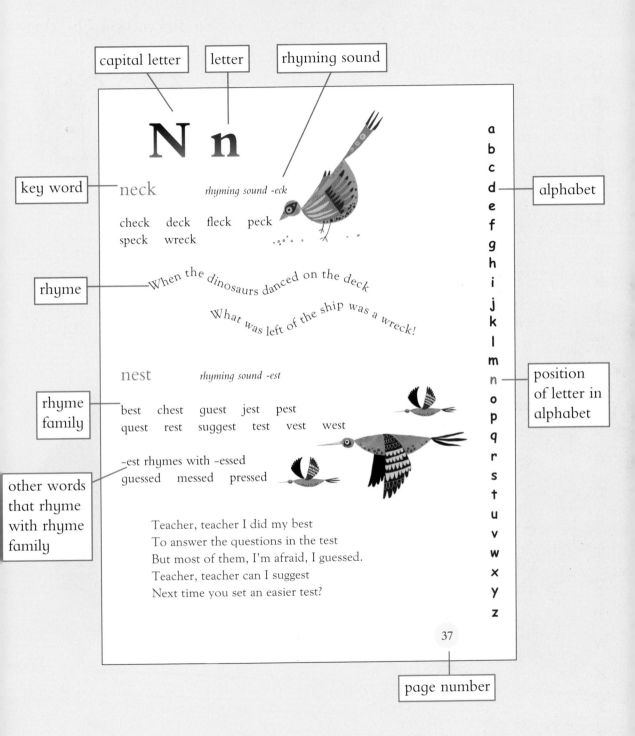

N n

key word — **neck** *rhyming sound -eck*

check   deck   fleck   peck
speck   wreck

rhyme — When the dinosaurs danced on the deck
What was left of the ship was a wreck!

nest *rhyming sound -est*

rhyme family — best   chest   guest   jest   pest
quest   rest   suggest   test   vest   west

other words that rhyme with rhyme family — –est rhymes with –essed
guessed   messed   pressed

Teacher, teacher I did my best
To answer the questions in the test
But most of them, I'm afraid, I guessed.
Teacher, teacher can I suggest
Next time you set an easier test?

alphabet — a b c d e f g h i j k l m n o p q r s t u v w x y z — position of letter in alphabet

37 — page number

7

a b c d e f g h i j k l m n o p q r s t u v w x y z

A a

ape *rhyming sound -ape*

cape   escape   grape   scrape
shape   tape

An ape in a cape
Has made an escape from the zoo.
If you see an ape in a cape
We'd like to hear from you.

arm *rhyming sound -arm*

alarm   charm

farm   harm

-arm rhymes with -alm
calm   palm

B b

back   *rhyming sound -ack*

black   crack   Jack   pack   quack   rack   sack
smack   snack   stack   track

There was a young fellow called Jack
Who jumped on a donkey's back
    When he gave it a smack
    It reared its back
And tossed Jack onto the track.

bag   *rhyming sound -ag*

brag   crag   drag   flag   nag   rag
sag   snag   stag   tag   wag

When Mum picks up her bag
    Our dog's tail starts to wag
        Back and forth like a flag.

a
b
c
d
e
f
g
h
i
j
k
l
m
n
o
p
q
r
s
t
u
v
w
x
y
z

ball *rhyming sound -all*

all   call   fall   football
hall   small   stall   tall   wall

-all rhymes with -awl
crawl   scrawl   sprawl

I spent hours kicking a ball
At a goal that was drawn on a wall
Without scoring a goal at all
'Cause the goal on the wall was too small!

bang *rhyming sound -ang*

clang   fang   gang   hang
rang   sang   sprang   tang   twang

bed

rhyming sound -ed

bled   fed   fled   led
red   shed   sled   Ted   wed

-ed rhymes with some -ead words
bread   dead   head   lead   read
spread   thread   tread

Another word that rhymes with bed is
said

Bouncing Ben bounced on the bed
Bounced to the ceiling and bumped his head.

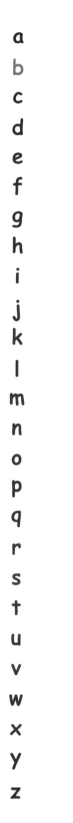

boat *rhyming sound -oat*

coat   float   gloat   goat   moat
oat   throat

-oat rhymes with -ote
note   vote   wrote

book *rhyming sound -ook*

brook   cook   crook   hook   look
rook   shook   took

breeze *rhyming sound -eeze*

freeze   sneeze   wheeze

-eeze rhymes with -ees
bees   chimpanzees   knees   trees

Other words that rhyme with breeze
cheese   these   fleas   teas   please

Chimpanzees sit up in trees
Picking fleas from off their knees.

a b c d e f g h i j k l m n o p q r s t u v w x y z

C c

cage   *rhyming sound -age*

age   page   rage   stage   wage

cake   *rhyming sound -ake*

bake   brake   fake   flake   lake
make   mistake   quake   rake
shake   snake   stake   take   wake

Some -eak words rhyme with cake
break   steak

camp   *rhyming sound -amp*

champ   clamp   cramp   damp   lamp
ramp   scamp   stamp   tramp

a
b
c
d
e
f
g
h
i
j
k
l
m
n
o
p
q
r
s
t
u
v
w
x
y
z

a
b
c
d
e
f
g
h
i
j
k
l
m
n
o
p
q
r
s
t
u
v
w
x
y
z

car   *rhyming sound -ar*

bar   far   guitar   jar   scar
spar   star   tar

Other words that rhyme with car
pa   ma   are

I want to be a TV star.
I want to play a flash guitar.
I want to be a TV star!
I want to drive a racing car.
I want to be the best by far.

chip   *rhyming sound -ip*

clip   dip   drip   flip   grip
hip   lip   nip   pip   rip   sip
ship   skip   slip   snip   strip   tip
trip   whip   zip

clock

rhyming sound -ock

block   dock   flock   frock   knock
lock   rock   shock   sock

Knock knock! What a shock!
    Look at the clock – eight o'clock!
Grab your vest. Grab your frock.
    Grab your shoe. Grab your sock.
Slam the door. Lock the lock.
    Hurry! Hurry! Round the block.
Get to school by nine o'clock.
    What a morning! What a shock!
If you don't get up at Mum's first knock.

cow

rhyming sound -ow

allow   bow   brow   how   now
row   wow

cup

rhyming sound -up

pup   sup   up

a
b
c
d
e
f
g
h
i
j
k
l
m
n
o
p
q
r
s
t
u
v
w
x
y
z

D d

dad   *rhyming sound -ad*

bad   glad   had   lad   mad
pad   sad

Another word that rhymes with dad is
add

dog   *rhyming sound -og*

bog   cog   flog   fog   frog
hog   jog   log

I tripped over my dog in the fog.
I fell into a bog and frightened a frog.

dream

rhyming sound -eam

beam   cream   scream   steam
stream   team

-eam rhymes with -eem
seem

I scream. We all scream.

It's snowing, It's snowing, It's snowing, ice cream.

a
b
c
d
e
f
g
h
i
j
k
l
m
n
o
p
q
r
s
t
u
v
w
x
y
z

dress   *rhyming sound -ess*

address   bless   chess   guess   less   mess
press   stress

I've made a mess. I've made a mess.
I've spilt my drink all down my dress.
It'll need a clean. It'll need a press.
I've made a mess. I've spoiled my dress.

duck   *rhyming sound -uck*

buck   chuck   cluck   luck   muck
pluck   struck   stuck   suck   truck   yuck

E e

ear   *rhyming sound -ear*

clear   dear   fear   gear   hear   near   tear

-ear rhymes with -eer
beer   cheer   deer

Other words that rhyme with ear
here   pier

Oh dear, I can't hear.
You're not very clear.
You'll have to come near.
I fear that I've got
A flea in my ear!

a
b
c
d
e
f
g
h
i
j
k
l
m
n
o
p
q
r
s
t
u
v
w
x
y
z

end   *rhyming sound -end*

bend   blend   friend   lend   mend
pretend   send   spend   tend   trend

I'm at my wit's end with my friend.
Whenever we play "Let's pretend"
She wants to be boss.
It makes me so cross.
It's driving me round the bend.

F f

face   *rhyming sound -ace*

ace   Grace   lace   pace   place
space   trace   race

I took my place beside Grace
At the start of the three-legged race
  But my lace came undone
  When we started to run
And Grace fell flat on her face!

a
b
c
d
e
f
g
h
i
j
k
l
m
n
o
p
q
r
s
t
u
v
w
x
y
z

a
b
c
d
e
f
g
h
i
j
k
l
m
n
o
p
q
r
s
t
u
v
w
x
y
z

fish   *rhyming sound -ish*

dish   fish   swish   wish

five   *rhyming sound -ive*

alive   arrive   dive   drive   hive
jive   live

fox   *rhyming sound -ox*

box   ox

-ox rhymes with -ocks
blocks   clocks   docks
flocks   frocks   knocks
locks   rocks
shocks   socks

A
fox
in
a
box
wearing
stripy
socks.

G g

game

rhyming sound -ame

blame   came   dame   fame   flame
frame   lame   name   same
shame   tame

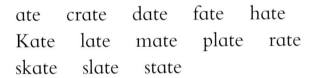

gate

rhyming sound -ate

ate   crate   date   fate   hate
Kate   late   mate   plate   rate
skate   slate   state

-ate rhymes with -ait
bait   wait

Other words that rhyme with gate
eight   weight
great   straight   fete

a
b
c
d
e
f
g
h
i
j
k
l
m
n
o
p
q
r
s
t
u
v
w
x
y
z

gold   *rhyming sound -old*

bold   cold   fold   hold   old
scold   sold   told

Let's play pirates!
I'll be the captain big and bold.
I'm in charge. You do as you're told.
You must give me all your gold.
Then I'll tie you up and throw you in the hold
While I sit in my cabin counting my gold.

grass   *rhyming sound -ass*

brass   class   glass   pass

H h

hair

rhyming sound -air

air   chair   fair   lair   pair   stair

-air rhymes with some –are words
bare   beware   care   dare   fare   hare   mare
rare   scare   spare

Other words that rhyme with hair
bear   pear   wear   their
there   where   prayer

hat

rhyming sound -at

at   bat   brat   cat   chat   fat
flat   gnat   mat   pat   rat
sat   spat   splat   that

hen   *rhyming sound -en*

Ben   den   Ken   Len   pen
ten   then   when

Another word that rhymes with hen is
again

There were two men called Ben and Ken.
Ben had a pig. Ken had a hen.
Ben swapped his pig for Ken's hen.
Then they swapped them back again
Again, again, again and again.
Now who's got the hen, Ben or Ken?

hill   *rhyming sound -ill*

bill   chill   drill   fill   grill   ill   Jill   kill
mill   pill   skill   spill   still   thrill   till   will

Jack and Jill went up the hill. "Wait there, Jack," said Jill. Jill ran off down the hill. And Jack is up there still!

hole

rhyming sound -ole

mole   pole   role   stole   vole   whole

-ole rhymes with -oal
foal   goal

Other words that rhyme with hole
bowl   roll   stroll   troll

Beneath the bridge is a deep, dark hole
In which there lives a terrible troll.

hut

rhyming sound -ut

but   cut   gut   jut   nut
rut   shut   strut

a
b
c
d
e
f
g
h
i
j
k
l
m
n
o
p
q
r
s
t
u
v
w
x
y
z

a
b
c
d
e
f
g
h
i
j
k
l
m
n
o
p
q
r
s
t
u
v
w
x
y
z

I i

ice   *rhyming sound -ice*

advice   dice   lice   mice   nice   price
rice   slice   spice   twice

Three blind mice didn't listen to advice
Went skating on the pond …

… and fell …

… through the …

… ice.

ink   *rhyming sound -ink*

blink   brink   chink   clink   drink
link   mink   pink   rink   shrink   sink
stink   think   wink

28

J j

jam   *rhyming sound -am*

am   cram   dam   exam   gram
ham   Pam   pram   ram   Sam
scram   slam   swam   tram
wham   yam

Another word that rhymes with jam is
lamb

jug   *rhyming sound -ug*

bug   chug   drug   dug   glug
hug   mug   plug   rug   shrug
slug   smug   snug   thug   tug

Said the slug in the jug
    To the bug in the rug
        "I'm not very snug in this jug.
            Are you snug in your rug?"
                "I am," said the bug, feeling smug.

jump   *rhyming sound -ump*

bump   clump   dump   hump   lump
plump   pump   slump   stump   thump

I tried to jump on a camel's hump.

Now I have a big lump

'Cause I fell on the ground with a thump!

K k

kick   *rhyming sound -ick*

brick   chick   click   flick   lick   pick
quick   sick   stick   thick   tick   trick

Lick
a lolly
on a
stick!
Lick it
fast! Lick
it
quick!

king   *rhyming sound -ing*

bring   cling   ding   ping   ring
sing   spring   sting   string   swing
thing   wing

If I had a magic ring
I could wish for anything:
To swing on a star on a silver string
To dance with fairies in the spring
To sing and fly like a bird on the wing
To live in a palace like a king.

knit   *rhyming sound -it*

bit   exit   fit   flit   grit   hit   kit   lit   pit
sit   slit   spit   split   twit

L l

lid
rhyming sound -id

bid   did   forbid   grid   hid   kid
rid   skid   slid

light
rhyming sound -ite

bright   fight   flight   fright   knight
might   night   right   sight   tight

-ight rhymes with -ite
bite   kite   quite   white   write

lunch
rhyming sound -unch

bunch   crunch   hunch   munch
punch   scrunch

There's a rabbit in the dinner queue
    So I've got a hunch
        We'll have a bunch of carrots
            To munch for our lunch.

a b c d e f g h i j k l m n o p q r s t u v w x y z

33

M m

map *rhyming sound -ap*

bap   cap   chap   clap   flap
gap   lap   nap   rap   sap
scrap   slap   snap   strap   tap
trap   wrap   yap   zap

match *rhyming sound -atch*

batch   catch   hatch   latch   patch
scratch   snatch

meat *rhyming sound -eat*

beat   bleat   cheat   eat   feat
heat   neat   seat   treat   wheat

-eat rhymes with -eet
feet   greet   meet
sheet   street   sweet

moon

rhyming sound -oon

afternoon   baboon   balloon
cartoon   noon   soon   spoon

-oon rhymes with –une
June   tune

A
baboon flew
up to the moon.
"Go away!" said the
Man in the Moon
And he burst
the baboon's
balloon.

a
b
c
d
e
f
g
h
i
j
k
l
m
n
o
p
q
r
s
t
u
v
w
x
y
z

mud   *rhyming sound -ud*

bud   cud   dud   spud   stud   sud   thud

Other words that rhyme with mud
blood   flood

> After the storm there was a flood.
> I went in the garden and played in the mud.
> I got mud in my pants. I got mud in my hair.
> I got myself muddy everywhere.

mum   *rhyming sound -um*

drum   gum   glum   plum   strum
sum   yum

Other words that rhyme with mum
crumb   dumb
numb   thumb
come   some

When he stuck in his thumb
And pulled out a plum
Little Jack Horner looked glum.
'Cause he'd wanted some bubblegum.

N n

neck   *rhyming sound -eck*

check   deck   fleck   peck
speck   wreck

When the dinosaurs danced on the deck
What was left of the ship was a wreck!

nest   *rhyming sound -est*

best   chest   guest   jest   pest
quest   rest   suggest   test   vest   west

-est rhymes with -essed
guessed   messed   pressed

Teacher, teacher I did my best
To answer the questions in the test
But most of them, I'm afraid, I guessed.
Teacher, teacher can I suggest
Next time you set an easier test?

a
b
c
d
e
f
g
h
i
j
k
l
m
n
o
p
q
r
s
t
u
v
w
x
y
z

net   *rhyming sound -et*

bet   forget   fret   get   jet   let   met   pet
set   upset   vet   wet   yet

Other words that rhyme with net
sweat   threat

My dragon came out in a sweat
So I took him to see the vet.
When he saw the vet
He got really upset.
He took off like a jet
And hasn't come back yet.

nine   *rhyming sound -ine*

dine   fine   line   mine   pine   shine
spine   whine   wine

nose   *rhyming sound -ose*

chose   close   hose   pose   those

-ose rhymes with some -ows words
blows   bows   crows   flows   glows   grows   knows
mows   rows   shows   slows   snows   throws   tows

Other words that rhyme with nose
doze   froze
goes   hoes   toes
sews

The snowman says:
I like it when the north wind blows
And it snows and it freezes
My nose and my toes.

a
b
c
d
e
f
g
h
i
j
k
l
m
n
o
p
q
r
s
t
u
v
w
x
y
z

a
b
c
d
e
f
g
h
i
j
k
l
m
n
o
p
q
r
s
t
u
v
w
x
y
z

O o

oil
rhyming sound -oil

boil   coil   foil   soil   spoil

out
rhyming sound -out

about   scout   shout   snout   sprout
stout   trout

P p

park

rhyming sound -ark

ark   bark   dark   hark   lark   mark   shark   spark

If you go for a walk in the park after dark
You can hear the ghost dogs bark.

pin

rhyming sound -in

bin   chin   din   fin   grin   in   robin   shin
skin   sin   thin   tin   twin   win

pool

rhyming sound -ool

cool   fool   school   stool   tool

-ool rhymes with –ule
mule   rule

A mule playing the fool in the swimming pool.

pot   *rhyming sound -ot*

blot   cot   dot   forgot   got
hot   jot   knot   lot   not
plot   rot   Scot   shot
spot   tot   trot

pull   *rhyming sound -ull*

bull   full

Another word that rhymes with pull is
wool

How now, brown cow
What's that you pull?
Is it a wagon full of finest wool?

No, it's full of turnips
and I'm a **bull!**

Q q

queen   *rhyming sound -een*

been   green   keen
screen   seen

-een rhymes with -ean
bean   clean   Jean
lean   mean

Jean, Jean dressed in green
Jean, Jean where have you been?
I've been up to London to visit
the queen.

Jean, Jean dressed in green
Was that you on the TV screen?
Yes it was! It was me with the queen!

R r

ride   *rhyming sound -ide*

bride   glide   guide   hide   side
slide   tide   wide

-ide rhymes with -ied
cried   died   dried   fried
lied   spied   tied   tried

room   *rhyming sound -oom*

bloom   boom   broom   doom
gloom   groom   loom   zoom

Zoom round the room.

Flash!

Crash!

Boom!

Here I go on my supersonic broom!

rope   *rhyming sound -ope*

cope   hope   mope   pope   slope

Another word that rhymes with rope is
soap

Slippery soap, slippery soap

You haven't a hope

Of

catching

the

soap.

round   *rhyming sound -ound*

around   bound   found
ground   hound   mound
pound   sound

a
b
c
d
e
f
g
h
i
j
k
l
m
n
o
p
q
r
s
t
u
v
w
x
y
z

S s

a
b
c
d
e
f
g
h
i
j
k
l
m
n
o
p
q
r
s
t
u
v
w
x
y
z

sand   *rhyming sound -and*

band   grand   hand   land   stand

seed   *rhyming sound -eed*

bleed   feed   need   speed   weed

-eed words rhyme with some -ead words
bead   lead   read

There was a young wizard called Reed
Who planted a new type of seed.
He chanted a spell to make it grow well
And it grew and it grew at great speed.
It grew tall as a tower, and gave him great power.
He had grown a magical weed.

46

sheep

rhyming sound -eep

beep   bleep   cheep   creep   deep   jeep
keep   peep   sleep   steep   sweep   weep

-eep rhymes with -eap
cheap   heap   leap

> At night when everyone's fast asleep
> Out from their cellars, dark and deep,
> The goblins creep.

shirt

rhyming sound -irt

dirt   skirt   squirt

-irt rhymes with -urt
hurt   spurt

shop

rhyming sound -op

chop   clop   drop   flop   hop
mop   pop   plop   stop   top

Don't
drop your
l o l l i p o p
Or your lolly
will go
p
l
o
p!

shore *rhyming sound -ore*

before   bore   core   chore
explore   more   score   store

-ore rhymes with -oar
boar   oar   roar   soar

-ore also rhymes with -aw
claw   draw   gnaw   jaw   law
paw   raw   saw   straw   thaw

Other words that rhyme with shore
door   floor
for   or   nor
four   pour   your
war   dinosaur

Dinah Shore dreamed she saw a dinosaur
Knock on her window with its claw.
Dinah Shore dreamed she saw a dinosaur
Peeping round her bedroom door.
Dinah Shore dreamed she saw a dinosaur
Fast asleep on the kitchen floor.
Dinah Shore dreamed she saw a dinosaur
Wake up and give a mighty **ROAR!**

a
b
c
d
e
f
g
h
i
j
k
l
m
n
o
p
q
r
s
t
u
v
w
x
y
z

six *rhyming sound -ix*

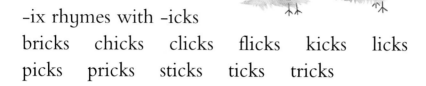

fix   mix

-ix rhymes with -icks
bricks   chicks   clicks   flicks   kicks   licks
picks   pricks   sticks   ticks   tricks

The magician flicks his wand
Clicks his fingers
And out of his empty hat he picks
Six fluffy little chicks.

smile *rhyming sound -ile*

crocodile   file   mile   pile   stile
tile   vile   while

Beware the smile of the crocodile
What he really wants to do
Is smile while he *is chewing you!*

snow

rhyming sound -ow

below	blow	bow	crow	flow
glow	grow	know	low	pillow
row	shadow	show	slow	sow
throw	window			

Other words that rhyme with snow

hoe	Joe	toe	hello
no	radio	so	
sew	though		

song

rhyming sound -ong

along	bong	dong	gong	long
pong	prong	strong	wrong	

Sing along! Sing a song!
Bing! Bang! Bong!
Sing along! Sing a song!
Ding! Dang! Dong!

a
b
c
d
e
f
g
h
i
j
k
l
m
n
o
p
q
r
s
t
u
v
w
x
y
z

spade   *rhyming sound -ade*

blade   fade   lemonade   made
marmalade   shade   trade   wade

-ade rhymes with -aid
afraid   laid   paid   raid

-ade also rhymes with -ayed
played   prayed   stayed

After we played we lay in the shade
Drinking **ICE-ICE-ICE**-cold lemonade.

speak   *rhyming sound -eak*

beak   creak   leak   peak   sneak
squeak   weak

-eak rhymes with -eek
leek   peek   seek   week

splash

rhyming sound -ash

ash   bash   cash   clash   crash   dash   flash
gash   lash   mash   rash   smash   thrash   trash

sport

rhyming sound -ort

fort   port   short   sort

-ort rhymes with -aught
caught   taught

Other words that rhyme with -ort
fought   nought   ought   thought

sun

rhyming sound -un

bun   fun   gun   nun
run   spun

-un rhymes with some -one words
done   none   one

-un words rhyme with some -on words
son   ton

a b c d e f g h i j k l m n o p q r s t u v w x y z

swim

rhyming sound -im

brim	dim	grim	him	Jim	Kim
prim	rim	skim	slim	Tim	trim

Slim Jim said to prim Kim
"Can you swim?"
"I can't," said prim Kim.
"But trim Tim can swim.
Can you swim as fast as him, Jim?"
"I can swim," said slim Jim
"But not as fast as trim Tim."

T t

tail   *rhyming sound -ail*

fail   frail   hail   jail   mail   nail
pail   rail   sail   snail   trail   wail

-ail rhymes with -ale
dale   gale   male   pale   sale   scale   stale
tale   whale

Dale told a tale
Of how he went for a sail
And caught a whale in a pail.

a
b
c
d
e
f
g
h
i
j
k
l
m
n
o
p
q
r
s
t
u
v
w
x
y
z

tank   *rhyming sound -ank*

bank   blank   clank   drank   Frank
plank   sank   shrank   spank   stank   thank

There once was a boy called Frank
    Who was fooling around on a plank.

He fell into a tank

And when he came out he stank!

tent   *rhyming sound -ent*

accident   bent   dent   event   lent
rent   scent   sent   spent   went

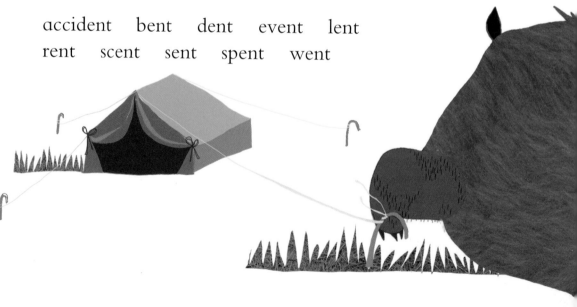

tie

rhyming sound -ie

die   lie   pie

-ie rhymes with some -y words
by   cry   dry   fly   fry   my   shy   sky   sly
spy   sty   try   why

-ie also rhymes with -igh
high   sigh   thigh

Other words that rhyme with -ie
dye   eye   buy   guy
bye   goodbye   I

time

rhyming sound -ime

chime   crime   grime
lime   mime   slime

Other words that rhyme with -ime
climb   rhyme

town   *rhyming sound -own*

brown   clown   crown   down   drown   frown   gown

A king with a golden crown,
A lady in a fine gown,
And a clown whose trousers have *fallen down!*

toy   *rhyming sound -oy*

annoy   boy   enjoy   Roy

train   *rhyming sound -ain*

again   brain   chain
drain   gain   main   pain
plain   rain   Spain   stain

-ain rhymes with -ane
cane   crane   Jane   lane
mane   pane   plane

tree

rhyming sound -ee

bee   flee   free   glee   knee
see   three

Other words that rhyme with –ee
flea   pea   sea   tea
he   me   she   we
chimney   key   monkey

U u

under   *rhyming sound -under*

blunder   thunder

Another word that rhymes with under is wonder

When thunder booms overhead
My little brother hides under the bed.

V v

van *rhyming sound -an*

an   can   fan   gran
man   nan   pan   plan
ran   Stan   than

Stan, Stan, the lollipop man
        Drives a blue and yellow van
And washes his socks in a frying pan.

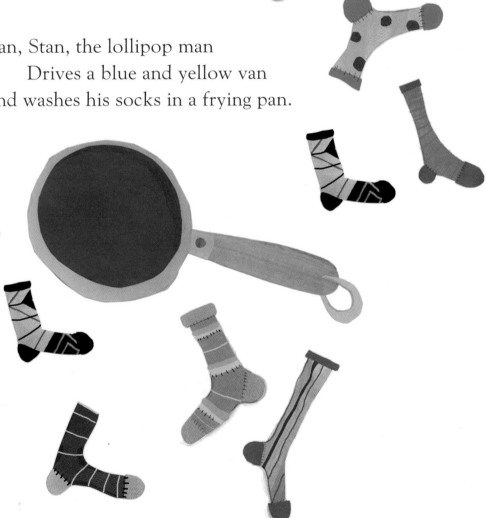

a
b
c
d
e
f
g
h
i
j
k
l
m
n
o
p
q
r
s
t
u
v
w
x
y
z

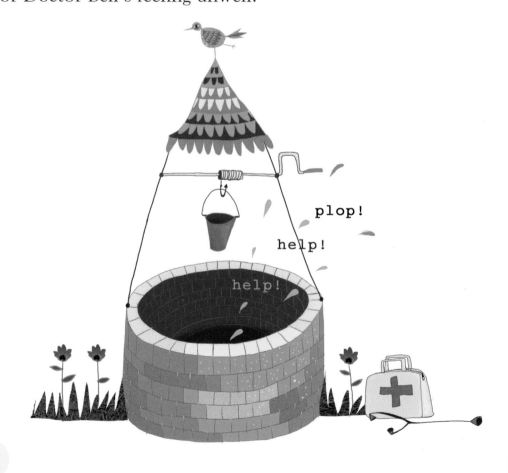

W w

well   *rhyming sound -ell*

bell   cell   dwell   fell   hell   sell
shell   spell   smell   tell   unwell   yell

With a yell Doctor Bell tripped and fell
Head first down into the well.
  Now he's lying in bed,
  Holding his head,
Poor Doctor Bell's feeling unwell.

plop!

help!

help!

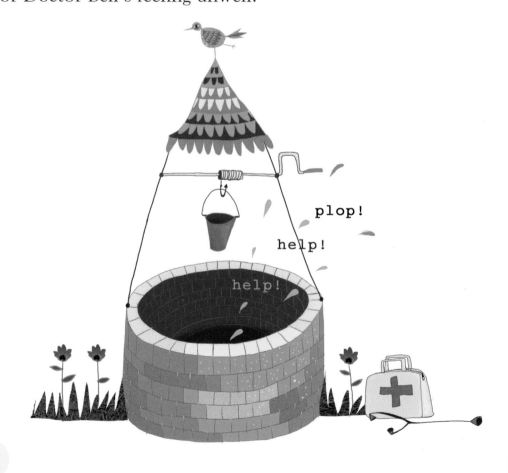

a
b
c
d
e
f
g
h
i
j
k
l
m
n
o
p
q
r
s
t
u
v
w
x
y
z

wheel

rhyming sound -eel

eel feel heel kneel peel
reel steel

-eel rhymes with -eal
deal heal meal real seal
squeal steal

I spin round and round on the Big Wheel. My stomach spins round and round and I feel I'm about to lose my last meal.

I spin round and round on the Big Wheel. My stomach spins round and round and I feel I'm about to lose my last meal.

wig   *rhyming sound -ig*

big   dig   fig   jig   pig   rig
swig   twig

A guinea pig
      ate a fig while
            an earwig danced a jig.

X x

X-ray   *rhyming sound -ay*

away   bay   bray   clay   day   hay   hurray
lay   may   pay   play   pray   ray   say   spray
stay   stray   sway   today   tray   way

-ay rhymes with -eigh
neigh   sleigh   weigh

-ay also rhymes with some -ey words
obey   prey   they

Y y

yard   *rhyming sound -ard*

card   hard   lard

Another word that rhymes with yard is
guard

I bought a postcard
    of them changing the guard
        in the palace yard.

a
b
c
d
e
f
g
h
i
j
k
l
m
n
o
p
q
r
s
t
u
v
w
x
y
z

Z z

ZOO   *rhyming sound -oo*

boo   kangaroo   moo

-oo rhymes with -ue
blue   glue   true

-oo also rhymes with some -ew words
blew   flew   grew   new

Other words that rhyme with zoo
do   to   you   two

"How do you do, Mr Kangaroo.
What are you doing out of the zoo
And why are you wearing one blue shoe?"

"I lost the other in a pot of glue
So I'm off to the shoe shop
To buy a new shoe.
Good day to you," said the kangaroo.

A to Z Index

B b

buck 18
bud 36
bug 29
bull 42
bump 30
bun 53
bunch 33
but 27
buy 57
by 57
bye 57

C c

cage **13**
cake **13**
call 10
calm 8
came 23
camp **13**
can 61
cane 58
cap 34
cape 8
car **14**
card 65
care 25
cartoon 35
cash 53
cat 25
catch 34
caught 53
cell 62
chain 58
chair 25

champ 13
chap 34
charm 8
chat 25
cheap 47
cheat 34
check 37
cheep 47
cheer 19
cheese 12
chess 18
chest 37
chick 32
chicks 50
chill 26
chime 57
chimney 59
chimpanzees 12
chin 41
chink 28
chip **14**
chop 47
chore 48
chose 39
chuck 18
chug 29
clamp 13
clang 10
clank 56
clap 34
clash 53
class 24
claw 48
clay 65
clean 43
clear 19

click 32
clicks 50
climb 57
cling 32
clink 28
clip 14
clock **15**
clocks 22
clop 47
close 39
clown 58
cluck 18
clump 30
coat 12
cog 16
coil 40
cold 24
come 36
cook 12
cool 41
cope 45
core 48
cot 42
cow **15**
crack 9
crag 9
cram 29
cramp 13
crane 58
crash 53
crate 23
crawl 10
creak 52
cream 17
creep 47
cried 44

crime 57
crocodile 50
crook 12
crow 51
crown 58
crows 39
crumb 36
crunch 33
cry 57
cud 36
cup **15**
cut 27

D d

dad **16**
dale 55
dam 29
dame 23
damp 13
dare 25
dark 41
dash 53
date 23
day 65
dead 11
deal 63
dear 19
deck 37
deep 47
deer 19
den 26
dent 56
dice 28
did 33

die 57
died 44
dig 64
dim 54
din 41
dine 39
ding 32
dinosaur 48
dip 14
dirt 47
dish 22
dive 22
do 66
dock 15
docks 22
dog 16
done 53
dong 51
doom 44
door 48
dot 42
down 58
doze 39
drag 9
drain 58
drank 56
draw 48
dream 17
dress 18
dried 44
drill 26
drink 28
drip 14
drive 22
drop 47
drown 58

drug 29
drum 36
dry 57
duck 18
dud 34
dug 29
dumb 36
dump 30
dwell 62
dye 57

E e

ear 19
eat 34
eel 63
eight 23
end 20
enjoy 58
escape 8
event 56
exam 29
exit 32
explore 48
eye 57

F f

face 21
fade 52
fail 55
fair 25
fake 13
fall 10
fame 23
fan 61
fang 10
far 14
fare 25
farm 8
fat 25
fate 23
fear 19
feat 34
fed 11
feed 46
feel 63
feet 34
fell 62
fete 23
fig 64
fight 33
file 50
fill 26
fin 41
fine 39
fish 22
fit 32
five 22
fix 50
flag 9
flake 13

flame 23
flap 34
flash 53
flat 25
flea 59
fleas 12
fleck 37
fled 11
flee 59
flew 66
flick 32
flicks 50
flight 33
flip 14
flit 32
float 12
flock 15
flocks 22
flog 16
flood 36
floor 48
flop 47
flow 51
flows 39
fly 57
foal 27
fog 16
foil 40
fold 24
fool 41
football 10
for 48
forbid 33
forget 38
forgot 42
fort 53

fought 53
found 45
four 48
fox 22
frail 55
frame 23
Frank 56
free 59
freeze 12
fret 38
fried 44
friend 20
fright 33
frock 15
frocks 22
frog 16
frown 58
froze 39
fry 57
full 42
fun 53

G g

gain 58
gale 55
game 23
gang 10
gap 34
gash 53
gate 23
gear 19
get 38
glad 16
glass 24

glee 59
glide 44
gloat 12
gloom 44
glow 51
glows 39
glue 66
glug 29
glum 36
gnat 25
gnaw 48
goal 27
goat 12
goes 39
gold 24
gong 51
goodbye 57
got 42
gown 58
Grace 21
gram 29
gran 61
grand 46
grape 8
grass 24
great 23
green 43
greet 34
grew 66
grey 65
grid 33
grill 26
grim 54
grime 57
grin 41
grip 14

grit 32
groom 44
ground 45
grow 51
grows 39
guard 65
guess 18
guessed 37
guest 37
guide 44
guitar 14
gum 36
gun 53
gut 27
guy 57

H h

had 16
hail 55
hair 25
hall 10
ham 29
hand 46
hang 10
hard 65
hare 25
hark 41
harm 8
hat 25
hatch 34
hate 23
hay 65
he 59
head 11

heal 63
heap 47
hear 19
heat 34
heel 63
hell 62
hello 51
hen 26
here 19
hid 33
hide 44
high 57
hill 26
him 54
hip 14
hit 32
hive 22
hoe 51
hoes 39
hog 16
hold 24
hole 27
hook 12
hop 47
hope 45
hose 39
hot 42
hound 45
how 15
hug 29
hump 30
hunch 33
hurray 65
hurt 47
hut 27

I i

I 57
ice 28
ill 26
in 41
ink 28

J j

Jack 9
jail 55
jam 29
Jane 58
jar 14
jaw 48
Jean 43
jeep 47
jest 37
jet 38
jig 64
Jill 26
Jim 54
jive 22
Joe 51
jog 16
jot 42
jug 29
jump 30
June 35
jut 27

K k

kangaroo 66
Kate 23
keen 43
keep 47
Ken 26
key 59
kick 32
kicks 50
kid 33
kill 26
Kim 54
king 32
kit 32
kite 33
knee 59
kneel 63
knees 12
knight 33
knit 32
knock 15
knocks 22
knot 42
know 51
knows 39

L l

lace 21
lad 16
laid 52
lair 25
lake 13
lamb 29

lame 23
lamp 13
land 46
lane 58
lap 34
lard 65
lark 41
lash 53
latch 34
late 23
law 48
lay 65
lead (as in bed) 11
lead (as in seed) 46
leak 52
lean 43
leap 47
led 11
leek 52
lemonade 52
Len 26
lend 20
lent 56
less 18
let 38
lice 28
lick 32
licks 50
lid 33
lie 57
lied 44
light 33
lime 57
line 39
link 28
lip 14

lit 32
live 22
lock 15
locks 22
log 16
long 51
look 12
loom 44
lot 42
low 51
luck 18
lump 30
lunch 33

M m

mad 16
made 52
mail 55
main 58
make 13
male 55
man 61
mane 58
map 34
mare 25
mark 41
marmalade 52
mash 53
mat 25
match 34
mate 23
may 65
me 59
meal 63

mean 43
meat 34
meet 34
mend 20
mess 18
messed 37
met 38
mice 28
might 33
mile 50
mill 26
mime 57
mine 39
mink 28
mistake 13
mix 50
moat 12
mole 27
monkey 59
moo 66
moon 35
mop 47
mope 45
more 48
mound 45
mows 39
muck 18
mud 36
mug 29
mule 41
mum 36
munch 33
my 57

N n

nag 9
nail 55
name 23
nan 61
nap 34
near 19
neat 34
neck 37
need 46
neigh 65
nest 37
net 38
new 66
nice 28
night 33
nine 39
nip 14
no 51
none 53
noon 35
nor 48
nose 39
not 42
note 12
nought 53
now 15
numb 36
nun 53
nut 27

O o

oar 48

oat 12
obey 65
oil 40
old 24
one 53
or 48
ought 53
out 40
ox 22

P p

pace 21
pack 9
pad 16
page 13
paid 52
pail 55
pain 58
pair 25
pale 55
palm 8
Pam 29
pan 61
pane 58
park 41
pass 24
pat 25
patch 34
paw 48
pay 65
pea 59
peak 52
pear 25
peck 37

peek 52
peel 63
peep 47
pen 26
pest 37
pet 38
pick 32
picks 50
pie 57
pier 19
pig 64
pile 50
pill 26
pillow 51
pin 41
pine 39
ping 32
pink 28
pip 14
pit 32
place 21
plain 58
plan 61
plane 58
plank 56
plate 23
play 65
played 52
please 12
plop 47
plot 42
pluck 18
plug 29
plum 36
plump 30
pole 27

sews 39
shade 52
shadow 51
shake 13
shame 23
shape 8
shark 41
she 59
shed 11
sheep 47
sheet 34
shell 62
shin 41
shine 39
ship 14
shirt 47
shock 15
shocks 22
shoe 66
shook 12
shop 47
shore 48
short 53
shot 42
shout 40
show 51
shows 39
shrank 56
shrink 28
shrug 29
shut 27
shy 57
sick 32
Sid 33
side 44
sigh 57

sight 33
sin 41
sing 32
sink 28
sip 14
sit 32
six 50
skate 23
skid 33
skill 26
skim 54
skin 41
skip 14
skirt 47
sky 57
slam 29
slap 34
slate 23
sled 11
sleep 47
sleigh 65
slice 28
slid 33
slide 44
slim 54
slime 57
slip 14
slit 32
slope 45
slow 51
slows 39
slug 29
slump 30
sly 57
smack 9
small 10

smash 53
smell 62
smile 50
smug 29
snack 9
snag 9
snail 55
snake 13
snap 34
snatch 34
sneak 52
sneeze 12
snip 14
snout 40
snow 51
snows 39
snug 29
so 51
soap 45
soar 48
sock 15
socks 22
soil 40
sold 24
some 36
son 53
song 51
soon 35
sort 53
sound 45
sow 51
space 21
spade 52
Spain 58
spank 56
spar 14

spare 25
spark 41
spat 25
speak 52
speck 37
speed 46
spell 62
spend 20
spent 56
spice 28
spied 44
spill 26
spine 39
spit 32
splash 53
splat 25
split 32
spoil 40
spoon 35
sport 53
spot 42
sprang 10
sprawl 10
spray 65
spread 11
spring 32
sprout 40
spud 36
spun 53
spurt 47
spy 57
squeak 52
squeal 63
squirt 47
stack 9
stag 9

toy **58**
trace 21
track 9
trade 52
trail 55
train 58
tram 29
tramp 13
trap 34
trash 53
tray 65
tread 11
treat 34
tree 59
trees 12
trend 20
trick 32
tricks 50
tried 44
trim 54
trip 14
troll 27
trot 42
trout 40
truck 18
true 66
try 57
tug 29
tune 35
twang 10
twice 28
twig 64

twin 41
twit 32
two 66

U u

under 60
unwell 62
up 15
upset 38

V v

van 61
vest 37
vet 38
vile 50
vole 27
vote 12

W w

wade 52
wag 9
wage 13
wail 55
wait 23
wake 13
wall 10
war 48
way 65

we 59
weak 52
wear 25
wed 11
weed 46
week 52
weep 47
weigh 65
weight 23
well 62
went 56
west 37
wet 38
whale 55
wham 29
wheat 34
wheel 63
wheeze 12
when 26
where 25
while 50
whine 39
whip 14
white 33
who 66
whole 27
why 57
wide 44
wig 64
will 26
win 41
window 51
wine 39
wing 32
wink 28
wish 22

won 53
wonder 60
wool 42
wound 45
wow 15
wrap 34
wreck 37
write 33
wrong 51
wrote 12

X x

X-ray 65

Y y

yam 29
yap 34
yard 65
yell 62
yet 38
you 66
your 48
yuck 18
yum 36

Z z

zap 34
zip 14
zoo 66
zoom 44

Index of Rhyming Sounds

-ace see face
-ack see back
-ad see dad
-add see dad
-ade see spade
-ag see bag
-age see cage
-aid (as in made) see spade
-aid (as in said) see bed
-aight see gate
-ail see tail
-ain (as in rain) see train
-ain (as in again) see hen
-air see hair
-ait see gate
-ake see cake
-ale see tail
-all see ball
-alm see arm
-am see jam
-amb see jam
-ame see game
-amp see camp
-an see van
-and see sand
-ane see train
-ang see bang
-ank see tank
-ap see map
-ape see ape
-ar (as in jar) see car
-ar (as in war) see car
-ard see yard
-are (as in scare) see hair
-are (as in are) see car
-ass see grass
-ark see park
-arm see arm
-ash see splash
-atch see match
-at see hat
-ate see gate

-aught see sport
-aur see shore
-aw see shore
-awl see ball
-ay see X-ray
-ayed see spade
-ayer see hair

-e see tree
-ea see tree
-ead (as in head) see bed
-ead (as in bead) see seed
-eak (as in beak) see speak
-eak (as in break) see cake
-eal see wheel
-eam see dream
-ean see queen
-eap see sheep
-ear (as in fear) see ear
-ear (as in bear) see hair
-eas see breeze
-eat (as in heat) see meat
-eat (as in sweat) see net
-eat (as in great) see gate
-eck see neck
-ed see bed
-ee see tree
-eed see seed
-eek see speak
-eel see wheel
-eem see dream
-een see queen
-eep see sheep
-eer see ear
-ees see breeze
-eese see breeze
-eet see eat
-eeze see breeze
-eigh see X-ray
-eight see gate
-eir see hair
-el see well

-en see hen
-end see end
-ent see tent
-ere (as in here) see ear
-ere (as in where) see hair
-ess see dress
-essed see nest
-est see nest
-et see net
-ete (as in fete) see gate
-ew (as in chew) see zoo
-ew (as in sew) see snow
-ews (as in sews) see nose
-ey (as in key) see tree
-ey (as in they) see X-ray

-ice see ice
-ick see kick
-icks see -ix
-id see lid
-ide see ride
-ie see tie
-ied see ride
-ier see ear
-ig see wig
-igh see tie
-ight see light
-ile see smile
-ill see hill
-im see swim
-imb (as in climb) see time

78

-ime see time
-in see pin
-ine see nine
-ing see king
-ink see ink
-ip see chip
-irt see shirt
-ish see fish
-it see knit
-ite see light
-ive see five
-ix see six

-o (as in slow) see snow
-oal see hole
-oap see rope
-oar see shore
-oat see boat
-ock see clock
-ocks see fox
-oe see snow
-oes see nose
-og see dog
-oil see oil
-old see gold
-ole see hole
-oll (as in roll) see hole
-ome see mum
-on (as in son) see -un
-onder see under
-one (as in one) see -un
-ong see song
-oo see zoo
-ood (as in blood) see mud
-ook see book
-ool (as in cool) see pool

-ool (as in wool) see pull
-oom see room
-oon see moon
-oor see shore
-op see shop
-ope see rope
-or see shore
-ore see shore
-ose see nose
-ort see sport
-ot see pot
-ote see boat
-ought see sport
-ound see round
-our (as in pour) see shore
-out see out
-ow (as in cow) see cow
-ow (as in snow) see snow
-own see town
-ows see nose
-oy see toy
-ox see fox
-oze see nose

-uck see duck
-ud see mud
-ue see zoo
-ug see jug
-ule see pool
-ull see pull

-um see mum
-umb see mum
-ump see jump
-un see sun
-unch see lunch
-under see under
-une see moon
-up see cup
-urt see shirt
-ut see hut
-uy see tie

-y see tie
-ye see tie
-yme see time

OXFORD
Dictionaries and Thesauruses
for home and school

Oxford Very First Dictionary

Oxford First Dictionary
Oxford First Thesaurus

Oxford Junior Illustrated Dictionary
Oxford Junior Illustrated Thesaurus

Oxford Junior Dictionary
Oxford Junior Thesaurus

Oxford Primary Dictionary
Oxford Primary Thesaurus

Oxford School Dictionary
Oxford School Thesaurus

Oxford Mini School Dictionary
Oxford Mini School Thesaurus

Oxford Student's Dictionary

Large print
Oxford English Dictionary for Schools
Oxford English Thesaurus for Schools